INCIDENT AT VICHY

BY ARTHUR MILLER

★

DRAMATISTS
PLAY SERVICE
INC.

★

D1206754

INCIDENT AT VICHY was first presented by the Repertory Theater of Lincoln Center For The Performing Arts at the ANTA Washington Square Theatre, in New York City, on December 3, 1964. It was directed by Harold Clurman; the production was designed by Boris Aronson; lighting was by Jean Rosenthal; and the costumes by Jane Greenwood. The cast, in order of appearance, was as follows:

LEBEAU, *A Painter*	Michael Strong
BAYARD, *An Electrician*	Stanley Beck
MARCHAND, *A Businessman*	Paul Mann
POLICE GUARD	Barry Primus
MONCEAU, *An Actor*	David J. Stewart
GYPSY	Harold Scott
A WAITER	Jack Waltzer
A BOY	Ira Lewis
A MAJOR	Hal Holbrook
FIRST DETECTIVE	Alek Primrose
OLD JEW	Will Lee
SECOND DETECTIVE	James Dukas
LEDUC, *A Doctor*	Joseph Wiseman
POLICE CAPTAIN	James Greene
VON BERG, *A Prince*	David Wayne
PROFESSOR HOFFMAN	Clinton Kimbrough
FERRAND, *A Café Proprietor*	Graham Jarvis
FOUR PRISONERS	Daniel Ades, Pierre Epstein, Tony Lo Bianco, John Vari

TIME: September, 1942. Late morning.

PLACE: A place of detention in Vichy, France.

The play will be given without intermission.

NOTE

The play can be produced more realistically, as it has been in England. That is, the single bench across the back of the stage is replaced by various kinds of seats—a small baggage wagon, a barrel, a fruit crate, etc., and the characters are thereby freed to move about, to group and regroup according to the demands of succeeding confrontations. The virtue of this mode is perhaps an increase in physical suspense and verisimilitude. What is lost, however, is a certain choral quality which, while more difficult to sustain, is less misleading as to the play's nature. It is not intended that the characterizations should exist for their own sakes, as in a realistic play; we shall never "know" them in that kind of detail, for these are people caught in an historic cul-de-sac, an emergency, when human beings reveal more or less what is relevant to the emergency and little more. Inevitably therefore, a certain metaphoric quality will emerge which physical realism tends to overwhelm. At the same time, realism tends to raise expectations which the play is not designed to fulfill.

However, there is a level at which the choral, metaphoric mode may be seen as a species of realism at the same time. If we understand that surrounding these people is a society either terrified of helping them, or indifferent, or actively hostile to them, it is clear that physical immobility is an actual imposition of that society, and equally, the human expression of an inwardness, a speaking-to-the-self. For the greater part of the speeches turn out to be self-addressed even as they appear to be outer-directed by the speaker. Each man here is trying, in one way or another, to make sense of the senseless and to hold his personality together in the face of an institutional terror whose aim is to dehumanize him. In short, the play is a collective, half-conscious striving toward awareness of what is really at stake here over and beyond the political crisis involved.

The realistic presentation, however, has a particular virtue aside from those mentioned, in that it may physically emphasize the evolution of Prince Von Berg's comprehension of the moral world which he had thought he understood, but which it turns out he had never even entered. By being able to move about, the Prince can silently enter into the dilemmas of the others in a more obvious way than is possible if they are all held to the single bench. In a certain sense all these voices are his, the conflicting lines of vision of a decent man in a world he never made, a world, nevertheless, for which he is responsible. The "spine" of the play, in fact, is the gradual awakening of Von Berg, and whatever the mode of production, this must be made clear from the moment of his entrance.

INCIDENT AT VICHY

Vichy, France, 1942. A place of detention.

At the R., a corridor leads to a turning and an unseen door to the street. Across the back is a structure with two grimy windowpanes in it—perhaps an office, in any case a private room with a door opening from it at the L.

A long bench stands in front of this room, facing an empty and large area whose former use is unclear but suggestive of a warehouse, perhaps, an armory, or a part of a railroad station not used by the public. Two small boxes stand apart on either side of the bench.

When light begins to rise, six men and a boy of fifteen are discovered on the bench in particular attitudes expressive of their personalities and functions, frozen there like a small orchestra at the moment before they begin to play.

As normal light comes on their positions flow out of the frieze. It appears that they do not know one another and are sitting like people thrown together in a public place, mutually curious but self-occupied. However, they are anxious and frightened and tend to make themselves small and unobtrusive. Only one, Marchand, a fairly well-dressed businessman, keeps glancing at his watch and bits of paper and calling cards he keeps in his pockets, and seems normally impatient.

Now, out of hunger and great anxiety, Lebeau, a bearded, unkempt man of twenty-five, lets out a dramatized blow of air and leans forward to rest his head on his hands. Others glance at him, then away. He is charged with the energy of fear, and it makes him seem aggressive.

LEBEAU. Cup of coffee would be nice. Even a sip.

(No one responds. He turns to Bayard beside him. Bayard is his age,

poorly but cleanly dressed, a certain muscular austerity in his manner. Lebeau speaks in a private undertone.)

Have you got any idea what's going on?

BAYARD. *(Shakes his head.)* I was walking down the street.

LEBEAU. Me, too. Something told me—don't go out today. So I went out. Weeks go by and I don't open the door. Today I go out. And I had no reason, I wasn't even going anywhere. *(Looks left and right to the others and to Bayard.)* They get picked up the same way?

BAYARD. *(Shrugs.)* I've only been here a couple of minutes myself— just before they brought you in.

LEBEAU. *(Looks to the others.)* Does anybody know anything?

(There are shrugs and nods negative. Lebeau looks at the walls, and then to Bayard.)

This isn't a police station, is it?

BAYARD. Doesn't seem so. It's just some building they're using, I suppose.

LEBEAU. *(Glancing about uneasily, curiously.)* It's painted like a police station, though. There must be an international police-paint, they're always the same color, everywhere. Like dead clams and a little yellow mixed in.

(Pause. He glances at the other silent men, and tries to silence himself, like them. But it's impossible, and he says to Bayard, with a nervous smile:)

You begin wishing you'd committed a crime, don't you? Something definite.

(Bayard is not amused, but not unsympathetic.)

BAYARD. Try to sit still. It's no good getting excited. We'll find out soon.

LEBEAU. It's just that I haven't eaten since three o'clock yesterday afternoon. Everything gets more vivid when you're hungry, you ever notice that?

BAYARD. I'd give you something but I forgot my lunch this morning. Matter of fact, I was just turning back to get it when they came up alongside me. Why'n't you try to sit back and calm down?

LEBEAU. I'm nervous... I mean I'm nervous anyway. *(With a faint, frightened laugh.)* I was even nervous before the war.

(His little smile vanishes. He shifts in his seat. The others wait with subdued anxiety. He notices the good clothes and secure manner of Marchand, who is at the head of the line nearest the door. Lebeau leans forward to attract him.)

Excuse me.

(Marchand does not turn to him. Lebeau makes a short, sharp, low whistle. Marchand, already offended, turns slowly to him.)

Is that the way they picked you up?—on the street? *(Marchand turns forward again without answering.)* Monsieur? *(Marchand still does not turn back to him.)* Well, Jesus, pardon me for living.

MARCHAND. It's perfectly obvious they're making a routine identification check-up.

LEBEAU. Oh?

MARCHAND. With so many strangers pouring into Vichy this past year there are probably a lot of spies and God knows what. It's just a check-up on our papers, that's all.

LEBEAU. *(Turns to Bayard, hopefully.)* You think so?

BAYARD. *(Shrugs, obviously he feels there is something more to it.)* I don't know.

MARCHAND. *(To Bayard.)* Why? There are thousands of people running around with false papers, we all know that. You can't permit such things in wartime. *(The others glance uneasily at Marchand, whose sense of security is thereby confined to him alone.)* Especially now with the Germans starting to take over down here, you have to expect things to be more strict, it's inevitable.

(A pause. Lebeau once again turns to Marchand.)

LEBEAU. You don't get any...special flavor, huh?

MARCHAND. What flavor?

LEBEAU. *(Glancing at the others.)* Well, like...some racial implication, for instance?

MARCHAND. I don't see anything to fear if your papers are all right.

(He turns front, concluding the conversation. Again silence. But Lebeau can't contain his anxiety. He studies Bayard's profile, then turns to the man on his other side and studies his. Then turning back to Bayard he says quietly:)

LEBEAU. Listen, you are…Peruvian, aren't you?

BAYARD. What's the matter with you, asking questions like that in here? *(He turns forward.)*

LEBEAU. What am I supposed to do, sit here like a dumb beast?!

BAYARD. Look, friend, it's no good getting hysterical.

LEBEAU. I think we've had it. I think all the Peruvians have had it in Vichy. *(Suppressing a shout.)* In 1939 I had an American visa. Before the invasion. I actually had it in my hand…

BAYARD. Calm down—this may all be routine.

(Slight pause. Then…)

LEBEAU. Listen…

(He leans in and whispers into Bayard's ear. Bayard glances toward Marchand, then shrugs to Lebeau.)

BAYARD. I don't know, maybe; maybe he's not.

LEBEAU. *(Desperately attempting familiarity.)* What about you?

BAYARD. Will you stop asking idiotic questions? You're making yourself ridiculous.

LEBEAU. *(Erupting.)* But I am ridiculous, aren't you? In 1939 we were all packed up for America. Suddenly my mother wouldn't leave the furniture. I'm here because of a brass bed and some fourth-rate crockery. And a stubborn, ignorant woman.

BAYARD. Yes, but it's not all that simple. You should try to think of why things happen. It helps to know the meaning of one's suffering.

LEBEAU. What meaning? If my mother…

BAYARD. It's not your mother. The monopolies got control of Germany. Big business is out to make slaves of everyone, that's why you're here.

LEBEAU. Well, I'm not a philosopher, but I know my mother, and that's why *I'm* here. You're like people who look at my paintings— "What does this mean, what does that mean? *Look* at it, don't ask what it means; you're not God, you can't tell what anything means. I'm walking down the street before, a car pulls up beside me, a man gets out and measures my nose; they measure my nose, my ears, my mouth, the next thing I'm sitting in a police station or whatever the hell this bloody place is—and in the middle of Europe, the highest peak of civilization! And you know what it means?—after the Romans and the Greeks and the Renaissance, and you know what this *means*?

BAYARD. You're talking utter confusion.

LEBEAU. *(In terror.)* Because I'm utterly confused! *(He suddenly springs up and shouts like a child.)* Goddamit, I want some coffee!

(The Police Guard appears at the end of the corridor, a revolver on his hip. He strolls down the corridor and meets Lebeau, who has come halfway up. Lebeau halts, returns to his place on the bench, and sits. The Guard starts to turn to go up the corridor when Marchand raises his hand.)

MARCHAND. Excuse me, Officer, is there a telephone one can use? I have an appointment at eleven o'clock and it's quite…

(The Guard simply walks up the corridor, turns the corner, and disappears. Lebeau looks toward Marchand and shakes his head, laughing silently.)

LEBEAU. *(To Bayard, sotto.)* Isn't it marvelous! Isn't it wonderful? The man is probably on his way to work in a German coal mine and he's worried about breaking an appointment. And people want realistic painting, you see what I mean? *(Slight pause.)* Did they measure your nose?—Could you at least tell me that?

BAYARD. No, they just stopped me and asked for my papers. I showed them and they took me in.

MONCEAU. *(Leans forward to address Marchand.)* I agree with you, Monsieur.

(Marchand turns to him. Monceau is a bright-eyed, cheerful man of twenty-eight. His clothes were elegant, now frayed. He holds a gray felt hat on his knee, his posture rather elegant.)

Vichy must be full of counterfeit papers. I think as soon as they start it shouldn't take long. *(To Lebeau.)* Try to settle down.

LEBEAU. *(To Monceau.)* Did they measure your nose?

MONCEAU. *(Disapprovingly.)* I think it'd be best if we all kept quiet.

LEBEAU. *(Looks around at all, then back to Monceau.)* What is it, my clothes? How do you know, I might be the greatest painter in France.

MONCEAU. For your sake, I hope you are.

LEBEAU. What a crew! I mean the animosity!

(Pause.)

MARCHAND. *(Leaning forward to see Monceau.)* You would think, though, that with the manpower shortage they'd economize on personnel. In the car that stopped me there was a driver, two French detectives, and a German official of some kind. They could easily have put a notice in the paper—everyone would have come here to present his documents. This way it's a waste of a whole morning. Never mind the embarrassment.

LEBEAU. Embarrassment? I'm not embarrassed. I'm *scared* to death. *(To Bayard.)* You embarrassed?

BAYARD. Look, if you can't be serious just leave me alone.

(Pause. The Gypsy, seated in a corner on the floor, plays a harmonica softly. Lebeau leans forward to see the Gypsy. Now he points.)

LEBEAU. Gypsy? *(Whistles.)* Hey, Gypsy?

GYPSY. *(Drawing closer a copper pot at his feet.)* Gypsy.

LEBEAU. *(To Monceau.)* Gypsies never have papers, why'd they bother him?

MONCEAU. In his case it might be some other reason. He probably stole that pot.

GYPSY. No. On the pavement. *(Raises the copper pot from between his feet.)* I mend, make nice. I sit down to mend. Come police. Pfft!

MARCHAND. But of course they'll tell you anything. *(To Gypsy, laughing familiarly.)* Right?

(Gypsy laughs hollowly and turns away to his own gloom.)

LEBEAU. That's a hell of a thing to say to him. Would you say that to a man with a crease in his trousers?

MARCHAND. They don't mind. In fact, they're proud of stealing. *(To Gypsy.)* Aren't you? *(Gypsy glances at him blankly.)* I've got a place in the country where they come every summer. I like them, personally, especially the music. We often listen to them around their campfires.

(He hums a phrase of Gypsy music, snapping his fingers over his head, and laughs.)

But they'll steal the eyes out of your head. *(To Gypsy.)* Right?

(Gypsy shrugs and kisses the air contemptuously.)

LEBEAU. Why shouldn't he steal? How'd you get *your* money?

MARCHAND. I happen to be in business.

LEBEAU. So what have you got against stealing?

BAYARD. Are you trying to provoke somebody? Is that it?

LEBEAU. Another businessman.

BAYARD. I happen to be an electrician. But a certain amount of solidarity wouldn't hurt right now.

LEBEAU. How about some solidarity with Gypsies? Just because they don't work nine to five?

THE WAITER. *(A small man, middle-aged, still wearing his apron.)* I know this one. I've made him go away a hundred times. He and his wife stand outside the café with a baby, and they beg. It's not even their baby.

LEBEAU. So what? They've still got a little imagination.

THE WAITER. Yes, but they keep whining to the customers through the shrubbery. People don't like it.

LEBEAU. You know?—You all remind me of my father. Always worshipped the hard-working Germans. And now you hear it all over France…we have to learn how to work like the Germans. Good God, don't you ever read history?—Whenever a people starts to work hard, watch out, they're going to kill somebody.

BAYARD. That depends on how production is organized. If it's for private profit, yes, but…

LEBEAU. What are you talking about, when did the Russians start getting dangerous? When they learned how to work. Look at the Germans—for a thousand years peaceful, disorganized people—they start working and they're on everybody's back. Nobody's afraid of the Africans, are they?—Because they don't work. Read the Bible—work is a curse, you're not supposed to worship work.

MARCHAND. And how do you propose to produce anything?

LEBEAU. Well, that's the problem. *(Marchand and Bayard laugh.)* What's so funny?—*That is the problem!* Yes! To work without making work a god! What kind of crew is this!

(The office door opens and the Major comes out. He is twenty-eight, a wan but well-built man, something ill about him. He walks with a slight limp, and passing the line of men as he goes toward the corridor…)

THE WAITER. Good morning, Major.

(Startled, the Major nods to the Waiter.)

MAJOR. Oh. Good morning.

(He continues up the corridor, where he summons the Guard from around the corner—the Guard appears and they talk unheard.)

MARCHAND. *(Sotto.)* You know him?

THE WAITER. *(Proudly.)* Know him? I serve him breakfast every morning. Tell you the truth he's really not a bad fellow. Regular army, see, not one of these S.S. bastards. Got wounded somewhere, so they stuck him back here. Only came about a month ago, but he and I…

(The Major comes back down the corridor. The Guard returns to his post out of sight at the corridor's end. As he passes Marchand…)

MARCHAND. *(Leaping up and going to the Major.)* Excuse me, sir.

(Major slowly turns his face to Marchand. Marchand affects to laugh deferentially.)

I hate to trouble you but I would be much obliged if I could use a telephone for one minute. In fact, it's business connected to the food supply. I am the manager of…

(He starts to take out a business card, but the Major has turned away and walks to the door. But there he stops and turns back.)

MAJOR. I'm not in charge of this procedure. You will have to speak to the Captain of Police.

(He goes into the office.)

MARCHAND. I beg your pardon.

(The door has been closed on his line. Marchand goes back to his place and sits, glaring at the Waiter.)

THE WAITER. He's really not a bad fellow. *(They all look at him, eager for some clue.)* He even comes at night sometimes, you want to hear him play the piano. Gives himself French lessons out of a book. Always has a few nice words to say, too.

LEBEAU. Does he know that you're a…Peruvian?

BAYARD. *(Instantly.)* Don't discuss that here, for God's sake! What's the matter with you?

LEBEAU. Can't I at least find out what's going on? If it's a general identity check it's one thing, but if…

(From the end of the corridor enter—1st Detective with the Old Jew, a man in his seventies, bearded, carrying a large sackcloth bundle. Then 2nd Detective, holding the arm of Leduc. The Vichy Police Captain, uniformed, with Von Berg. And finally Professor Hoffman in civilian clothes. The Old Jew is directed to sit by the 1st Detective, and he does at the end of the bench. 2nd Detective directs Von Berg to sit beside the Old Jew. Only now does 2nd Detective release his hold on Leduc and indicates for him to sit beside Von Berg.)

2ND DETECTIVE. *(To Leduc.)* Don't you give me any more trouble now.

(The door opens and the Major enters. Instantly Leduc is on his feet, approaching the Major.)

LEDUC. Sir, I must ask the reason for this. I am a combat officer, captain in the French Army. There is no authority to arrest me in French territory. The Occupation has not revoked French law in Southern France.

(2nd Detective, infuriated, throws Leduc back into his seat. He returns to the Professor.)

2ND DETECTIVE. *(To Major of Leduc.)* Speechmaker.

PROFESSOR. *(Doubtfully, to the two detectives.)* You think you two can carry on now?

2ND DETECTIVE. We got the idea, Professor. There's certain

15

neighborhoods they head for when they run away from Paris or wherever they come from. I can get you as many as you can handle.

1ST DETECTIVE. It's a question of knowing the districts, you see. In my opinion you've got at least a couple of thousand more in Vichy on false papers.

PROFESSOR. You go ahead then.

(As 2nd Detective turns to go with 1st Detective, the Police Captain calls him.)

POLICE CAPTAIN. Saint-Pere.

2ND DETECTIVE. Yes, sir.

POLICE CAPTAIN. *(Walks D. with Detective.)* Try to avoid taking anybody out of a crowd. Just cruise around the way we did before, and take them one at a time. We don't want to alarm people.

2ND DETECTIVE. Yes, sir.

(The Captain gestures and both detectives leave up the corridor.)

POLICE CAPTAIN. I am just about to order coffee, will you gentlemen have some?

PROFESSOR. Please.

THE WAITER. *(Timidly.)* And a croissant for the Major.

(The Major glances quickly at the Waiter and barely smiles. The Police Captain, who has thrown a mystified look at the Waiter, goes into the office.)

MARCHAND. *(To Professor.)* I believe I am first, sir.

PROFESSOR. Yes, this way.

(He goes into the office, followed by the eager Marchand.)

MARCHAND. *(Going in.)* Thank you. I'm in a dreadful hurry... I was on my way to the Ministry of Supply, in fact... *(His voice is lost within.)*

(As the Major reaches the door, Leduc, who has been in a fever of calculation, calls to him.)

LEDUC. Amiens.

(Major halts at the door, turns to Leduc, who is at the far end of the line.)

MAJOR. Amiens, what about Amiens?

LEDUC. *(Suppressing his nervousness.)* July 9th, '40. I was in the 16th Artillery, facing you. I recognized your insignia, which of course I could hardly forget.

MAJOR. That was a bad day for you fellows.

LEDUC. Yes, it was. And evidently for you, too.

MAJOR. *(Glances down at his leg.)* Can't complain.

(Major goes into the office, shuts the door. A pause.)

WAITER. I told you he was all right—you'll see.

LEDUC. *(To all.)* What's this all about?

MONCEAU. *(To Leduc.)* It seems they're checking on identification papers.

(Leduc receives the news, and obviously grows cautious and quietly alarmed. He examines their faces.)

LEDUC. What's the procedure?

MONCEAU. They've just started—that businessman was the first.

LEBEAU. *(To Leduc and Von Berg.)* They measure your noses?

(Von Berg smiles incredulously.)

LEDUC. *(Sharply alarmed.)* Measure noses?

LEBEAU. *(Putting thumb and forefinger against the bridge and tip of his nose.)* Ya, they measured my nose, right there on the street. I tell you what I think... *(To Bayard.)* With your permission.

BAYARD. I don't mind you talking as long as you're serious.

LEBEAU. I think it's to carry stones. It just occurred to me—last Monday a girl I know came up from Marseilles—the road is full of detours. They probably need workers. There was a crowd of people, hundreds, just carrying stones. She thought a lot of them were Jew... *(Breaks off at the inflammatory word.)*

LEDUC. I never heard of forced labor in the Vichy Zone. Is that going on here?

BAYARD. Where do you come from?

(Slight pause—Leduc decides whether to reveal.)

LEDUC. I live in the country. I don't get into town very often. There's been no forced labor decree, has there?

BAYARD. *(To all.)* Now listen. *(Everyone turns to his straightforward, certain tone.)* I'm going to tell you something but I don't want anybody quoting me. Is that understood? *(They nod. He glances at the door. Then to Lebeau.)* You hear what I said?

LEBEAU. Don't make me out some kind of an idiot. I know it's serious!

BAYARD. I work on the railway here. In the marshalling yards. We took in an express freight train yesterday. Fifty vans or more. The engine driver was Polish so I couldn't talk to him but one of the signalmen said he heard people inside.

LEDUC. Inside the vans?

BAYARD. Yes. It came from Toulouse. I heard there's been a quiet roundup of Jews in Toulouse the last couple of weeks. And what's a Polish engine driver doing on a train in Southern France? You understand?

LEDUC. Concentration camp.

MONCEAU. Why? A lot of people have been volunteering for work in Germany. That's no secret. They're doubling the ration for anybody who goes.

BAYARD. *(Quietly.)* The cars are locked on the outside. *(Slight pause.)* And they stink. You can smell the stench a hundred yards away. Babies are crying inside. You can hear them. And women. They don't lock in volunteers like that. I never heard of it.

(A long pause.)

LEDUC. But I've never heard of them applying the Racial Laws down here. It's still French territory, regardless of the Occupation— they've made a big point of that.

(Pause.)

BAYARD. The Gypsy bothers me.

LEBEAU. Why?

BAYARD. They're in the same category of the Racial Laws. Inferior.

(Leduc and Lebeau slowly turn to look at the Gypsy.)

LEBEAU. *(Turning back quickly to Bayard.)* Unless he really did steal that pot. *(Shunting stops.)*

18

BAYARD. Well, yes, if he stole the pot then of course he…

LEBEAU. *(Quickly to the Gypsy.)* Hey, listen.

(He gives a soft, sharp whistle; the Gypsy turns to him.) You steal that pot?

(The Gypsy's face is inscrutable. Lebeau is embarrassed to press this, and more desperate.) You did, didn't you?

GYPSY. No steal, no.

LEBEAU. Look, I've got nothing against stealing; *(Indicating the others.)* I'm not one of these types. I've slept in parked cars, under bridges—I mean to me all property is theft anyway so I've got no prejudice against you.

GYPSY. No steal.

LEBEAU. Look…I mean you're a Gypsy, so how else can you live, right?

THE WAITER. He steals everything.

LEBEAU. *(To Bayard.)* You hear? He's probably in for stealing, that's all.

GYPSY. Never steal—I do tricks—look.

(The Gypsy leaps up and gracefully does a series of backflips across the stage, coming to rest on the floor near Von Berg. He lightly applauds, then…)

VON BERG. Excuse me… *(They turn to him.)* Have you all been arrested for being Jewish?

(They are silent, suspicious and surprised. He realizes his blunder.)

I'm terribly sorry. I had no idea.

BAYARD. I said nothing about being Jewish. As far as I know nobody here is Jewish.

VON BERG. I'm terribly sorry.

(Silence, and the moment lengthens. In his embarrassment he laughs nervously.)

It's only that I…I was buying a newspaper and this gentleman came out of a car and told me I must have my documents checked. I…I had no idea.

(Silence. Hope is rising in them. Von Berg looks at all of them with

19

new interest.)

LEBEAU. *(To Bayard.)* So what'd they grab *him* for?

BAYARD. *(Looks at Von Berg for a moment, then at all.)* I don't understand it, but take my advice. If anything like that happens and you find yourself on that train…there are four bolts halfway up the doors on the inside. Try to pick up a nail or a screwdriver, even a sharp stone—you can chisel the wood out around those bolts and the doors will open. I warn you, don't believe anything they tell you—I heard they're working Jews to death in the Polish camps.

MONCEAU. I happen to have a cousin; they sent him to Auschwitz; that's in Poland, you know. I have several letters from him saying he's fine. They've even taught him bricklaying.

BAYARD. Look, chum, I'm telling you what I heard from people who know. *(Hesitates.)* People who make it their business to know, you understand? Don't listen to any stories about resettlement, or that they're going to teach you a trade or something. Wherever that train is going, get out before it gets there.

(Pause.)

LEDUC. I've heard the same thing. *(They turn to him and he turns to Bayard.)* Are there any tools round here that we could…

MONCEAU. This is so typical. We're in the French Zone, nobody has said one word to us, and we're already on a train for a concentration camp where we'll be dead in a year.

LEDUC. But if the engine driver is a Pole…

MONCEAU. All right, he's a Pole so what does that prove?

BAYARD. All I'm saying is that if you have some kind of tool…

LEDUC. I think what this man says should be taken seriously.

MONCEAU. In my opinion you're hysterical. After all, they were picking up Jews in Germany for years before the war, they've been doing it in Paris since they came in—are you telling me all those people are dead? Is that really conceivable to you? War is war, but you still have to keep a certain sense of proportion. I mean Germans are still *people*.

LEDUC. I don't speak this way because they're Germans.

BAYARD. It's because they're Fascists.

LEDUC. Excuse me, no. It's simply because they are people that I speak this way.

BAYARD. I don't agree with *that*.

MONCEAU. *(Looks at Leduc for an instant.)* You must have had a peculiar life is all I can say. I happen to have acted in Germany; I know the German people.

LEDUC. I studied in Germany for five years; I took my degree in Austria and I...

VON BERG. *(Happily.)* In Austria!—Where?

LEDUC. *(Again he hesitates, then reveals.)* The Medical School in Vienna—the Psychoanalytic Institute.

VON BERG. ...Really?

MONCEAU. No wonder you're so pessimistic—he's a psychiatrist!

VON BERG. Where did you live?—I am Viennese...

LEDUC. Excuse me, I think it's better not to speak too much in... detail.

VON BERG. *(Glancing about as though he had committed another gaffe.)* I'm terribly sorry...yes, of course. *(Slight pause.)* I was only curious to know if you were acquainted with Baron Kessler. He was very interested in the medical school.

LEDUC. *(With an odd coolness.)* Well, of course I've heard of him; but I was never in that circle.

VON BERG. Oh, he is very easy-going—very approachable. *(Shyly.)* ...He is my cousin.

LEBEAU. You're a nobleman?

VON BERG. Yes.

LEDUC. May I ask your name?

VON BERG. Wilhelm Johann Von Berg.

MONCEAU. *(Astonished, impressed.)* Prince Von Berg?

VON BERG. Yes...forgive me, have we met?

MONCEAU. *(Excited by the honor.)* Oh, no. But naturally I've heard your name. I believe it's one of the oldest houses in Austria.

VON BERG. Oh, that's of no importance anymore.

LEBEAU. *(Turning to Bayard—bursting with hope.)* Now what the hell would they want of an Austrian prince?!

(Bayard looks at Von Berg, mystified.)

I mean… *(Turning back to Von Berg.)* …you're Catholic, right?

VON BERG. Yes, I am.

LEDUC. But is your title on your papers?

VON BERG. On my passport, yes.

(Pause. They sit silent, on the edge of hope, but bewildered.)

MONCEAU. I told you. It's a general check-up on documents.

BAYARD. Were you…political or something?

VON BERG. No, no, I never had any interest in that direction.

(Slight pause.)

LEBEAU. There you are then.

VON BERG. Of course, there is this resentment of the aristocracy. That might explain it.

LEDUC. In the Nazis?—Resentment?

VON BERG. *(Surprised.)* Yes, certainly.

LEDUC. *(With no evident viewpoint, a neutral but pressing interest in drawing the nobleman out.)* Really. I've never been aware of that.

VON BERG. Oh, I assure you.

LEDUC. But on what ground?

VON BERG. *(Laughs, embarrassed to have to even suggest he is offended.)* You're not asking that seriously.

LEDUC. Don't be offended—I suppose our experience has been a bit different. I have taken for granted that the aristocracy is…always behind a reactionary regime.

VON BERG. A few individuals, certainly. But not people with a sense of their responsibilities.

LEDUC. That interests me. So you still take seriously the…the title and…

VON BERG. It is not a "title"; it is my name, my family. Just as you have a name, and a family. And you are not inclined to dishonor them, I presume.

LEDUC. That's good to hear. And by responsibility, you mean I suppose, that...

VON BERG. Oh, I don't know; whatever that means.

(Pause.)

LEDUC. Please forgive me, I'm simply ignorant of your situation. It should have been obvious— *(Pause.)* they *would* want to destroy whatever power you have.

VON BERG. Oh, no, I have no power. And if I did it would be a day's work for them to destroy it. That's not the issue.

(Leduc is fascinated. A pause. He is drawn to some truth in Von Berg.)

LEDUC. What is it, then?—Believe me, I'm not being critical. Quite the contrary...

VON BERG. But these are obvious answers! *(Laughs.)* I have a certain...standing. My name is a thousand years old and they know the disadvantage of someone like me is perhaps...not vulgar enough.

LEDUC. And by vulgar you mean...

VON BERG. Well, don't you think Nazism...whatever else it may be...is an outburst of vulgarity? An ocean of vulgarity?

BAYARD. I'm afraid it's a lot more than that, believe you me.

VON BERG. *(Politely to Bayard.)* I am sure it is, yes.

BAYARD. You make it sound like they have bad table manners, that's all.

VON BERG. They certainly do, yes. Nothing angers them more than a sign of any...delicacy. It is decadent, you see.

BAYARD. Are you trying to tell me you left Austria because of their table manners?

VON BERG. Table manners, yes; and their adoration of dreadful art; and grocery clerks in uniforms telling the orchestra what music it may not play. Vulgarity can be enough to drive a man out of his country, yes, I think so.

BAYARD. In other words, if they had good taste in art, and elegant table manners, and let the orchestra play whatever it liked, they'd be all right with you.

VON BERG. But how would that be possible? Can people with respect for art go about hounding Jews? Making a prison of Europe, pushing themselves forward as a race of policemen and brutes? Is that possible for artistic people?

MONCEAU. I'd like to agree with you, Prince Von Berg, but I have to say that the German audiences—I've played there—no audience is as sensitive to the smallest nuance of a performance; they sit in the theatre with respect; like in a church. And nobody listens to music like a German. Don't you think so? It's a passion with them.

VON BERG. *(Appalled at the truth; a pause.)* I'm afraid that is true, yes. *(Pause.)* I don't know what to say. *(He is depressed, deeply at a loss.)*

LEDUC. Perhaps it isn't that kind of person who's involved in this.

VON BERG. I'm afraid I know many cultured people who…did become Nazis. Yes, they did. Art is perhaps no defense against this. It's curious how one takes certain ideas for granted. Until this moment I had thought of art as a… *(To Bayard.)* You may be right—I don't understand very much about it.

LEDUC. Were you connected with the medical school?

VON BERG. I? Oh, no—I'm essentially a musician, in an amateur way of course…

(The office door opens and Marchand appears, backing out, talking to someone within. He is putting a leather document-wallet into his breast pocket, while with the other hand he holds a white pass.)

POLICE CAPTAIN. *(Unseen, within the office.)* All right, you can go now.

MARCHAND. *(Emerging.)* Thank you very much.

POLICE CAPTAIN. *(Within.)* Sorry you've been troubled.

MARCHAND. That's perfectly all right, I understand perfectly. Good day, gentlemen. *(Holding up the pass to them.)* I show the pass at the door?—Thank you. *(Shutting the door he turns and hurries past the line of prisoners, and as he passes the Boy…)*

THE BOY. What'd they ask you? Sir?

(Marchand turns up the corridor without glancing at the Boy, and as he approaches the end, the Guard, hearing him, appears there.

Marchand hands the pass to the Guard and goes out. The Guard moves around the turning of the corridor and disappears.)

LEBEAU. *(Half-mystified, half-hopeful.)* I could have sworn he was Jewish. *(To Bayard.)* Didn't you think so?

BAYARD. *(Slight pause.)* Yes, I did. You have papers, don't you?

LEBEAU. Oh, sure, I have marvelous papers. *(He takes rumpled documents out of his pants pocket.)*

BAYARD. Well, just insist they're valid. Maybe that's what he did.

LEBEAU. I wish you'd take a look at them, will you?

BAYARD. I'm no expert.

LEBEAU. I'd like your opinion, though; you seem to know what's going on. How they look to you?

(Bayard holds the paper up to the light, then quickly hides it as the office door opens. The Professor comes out with a clipboard holding a paper, which he studies. Now, finally, his eye falls on the Gypsy.)

PROFESSOR. Next. You. Come with me.

(The Gypsy gets up and starts toward him. Professor indicates the pot in the Gypsy's hand.)

You can leave that. *(The Gypsy hesitates, glances at the pot.)* I said leave it there.

GYPSY. Mend. No steal.

(The Professor simply looks at him. The Gypsy puts the pot down on the bench unwillingly.)

PROFESSOR. Go in.

GYPSY. *(To all, warningly, pointing at the pot.)* That's mine.

(The Gypsy goes into the office. The Professor follows him in and shuts the door. Bayard takes the pot and bends the handle off, gouges the bench to test it, and puts it in his pocket and sets the pot back where it was.)

VON BERG. *(Protesting Bayard's breaking off the handle.)* Excuse me!

LEBEAU. *(Ripping off the other handle and turning back to Bayard, indicating his paper.)* What do you think?

(Bayard holds the paper up to the light again, turns it over, gives it back to Lebeau.)

BAYARD. Looks good far as I can tell.

MONCEAU. That man did seem Jewish to me. Didn't he to you, Doctor?

LEDUC. I have no idea. Jews are not a race. They can look like anybody. *You* ought to know that.

LEBEAU. (*With the joy of near-certainty.*) He just probably had good papers. Because I know people have papers, I mean all you have to do is take one bleedin' look at them and you know the stamps are forged. But I mean if you've got good papers, right?

(*Monceau has meanwhile taken out his papers and is examining them. The Boy does the same with his. Lebeau turns to Leduc.*)

That's true, though. My father looks like an Englishman. The trouble is I took after my mother.

THE BOY. (*To Bayard, offering his paper.*) Could you look at mine?

(*Bayard examines the Boy's paper; his face shows it is an obvious forgery. He returns the paper.*)

BAYARD. I'm no expert, son. Anyway, don't stand there looking at it like that.

(*The Boy pockets the paper, he is more afraid now.*)

Look, if it's forced labor they might not take you; you're under sixteen, aren't you?

(*Monceau puts his own paper away. A pause. They wait.*)

MONCEAU. (*With a new anxiety, then more definitely.*) I think it's a question of one's credibility—that man just now did carry himself with a certain confidence…

(*The Old Jew begins to pitch forward onto the floor. Von Berg catches him and with the Boy helps him back onto the seat.*)

THE BOY. Doctor!

(*Leduc rushes over, tends to the old man.*)

LEBEAU. (*With heightened nervousness.*) God almighty, you'd think they'd shave off their beards. I mean walking around with a beard like that in a country like this! (*Monceau looks at his beard, and he—Lebeau—touches it…*) Well, I just don't waste time shaving, that's all, but…

VON BERG. *(To the Old Jew.)* Are you all right, sir?

(The Old Jew gestures to be left alone now.)

LEBEAU. Phew!

(Leduc bends over Von Berg's lap and feels the Old Jew's pulse. Pause. He lets his hand go, and looks toward Lebeau.)

LEDUC. Were you serious? They actually measured your nose?

LEBEAU. With his fingers. That civilian. They called him "professor." *(Pause; then to Bayard.)* I think you're right; it's all a question of your papers. That businessman certainly looked Jewish...

MONCEAU. I'm not so sure now.

LEBEAU. *(Angrily.)* A minute ago you were sure, now suddenly...

MONCEAU. Well, even if he didn't look Jewish—it only means it really is a general check-up. On the whole population.

LEBEAU. Hey, that's right, too! *(Slight pause.)* Actually, I'm often taken for a gentile myself. Not that I give a damn but most of the time, I... *(To Von Berg.)* How about you, they measure your nose?

VON BERG. No, they told me to get into the car, that was all.

LEBEAU. Because actually yours looks bigger than mine.

BAYARD. Will you lay off? Just lay off, will you?

LEBEAU. Can't I try to find out what I'm in for?

BAYARD. Did you ever think of anything beside yourself?—Just because you're an artist? You people demoralize everybody!

LEBEAU. *(With unconcealed terror.)* What the hell am I supposed to think of? Who're you thinking of?

(The office door opens. The Police Captain appears, gestures toward Bayard.)

POLICE CAPTAIN. Next—you—come inside.

(Bayard, trying hard to keep his knees from shaking, stands. Mr. Ferrand, the café proprietor, comes hurrying down the stairs with a tray of coffee-things covered with a large napkin. He has an apron on.)

FERRAND. Sorry, Captain.

POLICE CAPTAIN. Ah, at last!

FERRAND. Terribly sorry, but for you I had to make some fresh.

27

POLICE CAPTAIN. *(As he goes into the office behind Ferrand.)* Put it on my desk. *(The door is closed.)*

(Bayard sits, wipes his face. Pause.)

LEDUC. They seem to be keeping the Gypsy.

MONCEAU. *(To Bayard, quietly.)* Would you mind if I made a suggestion? *(Bayard turns to him, already defensive.)* You looked terribly uncertain of yourself when you stood up just now.

BAYARD. *(Taking offense.)* Me uncertain? You've got the wrong man.

MONCEAU. Please, I'm not criticizing you.

BAYARD. Naturally I'm a little nervous, facing a room full of Fascists like this.

MONCEAU. *(Always striving against his own breakdown.)* But that's why one must seem especially self-confident. I'm quite sure that's what got that businessman through so quickly. I've had similar experiences on trains, and even in Paris when they stopped me several times. The important thing is not to look like a victim. Or even to feel like one. They can be very stupid, but they do have a sense for victims; they know when someone has nothing to hide.

LEDUC. But how does one avoid feeling like a victim?

MONCEAU. One must create one's own reality in this world. I'm an actor, we do this all the time. The audience, you know, is very sadistic; it looks for your first sign of weakness. So you must try to think of something that makes you feel self-assured; anything at all. Like the day, perhaps, when your father gave you a compliment, or a teacher was amazed at your cleverness…any thought *(To Bayard.)* that makes you feel…valuable. After all, you are trying to create an illusion; to make them believe you are who your papers say you are.

LEDUC. I've never heard it put that way before. That's exactly the point. We must not play the part they have written for us. That's very wise. You must have great courage.

MONCEAU. I'm afraid not. But I have talent instead. *(To Bayard— encouraged by Leduc's agreement.)* One must show them the face of a man who is right, not a man who is suspect and wrong. They sense the difference.

BAYARD. My friend, you're in a bad way if you have to put on an act to feel your rightness. The bourgeoisie sold France; they let in the Nazis to destroy the French working class. Remember the causes of this war and you've got *real* confidence.

LEDUC. Excepting that the causes of this war keep changing so often.

BAYARD. Not if you understand the economic and political forces.

LEDUC. But when Germany attacked us the Communists refused to support France, didn't they? They pronounced it an imperialist war. Until the Nazis turned against Russia; then in one afternoon it all changed into a sacred battle against tyranny. What confidence can one feel from an understanding that turns upside-down in an afternoon?

BAYARD. Look, mate, without the Red Army standing up to them right this minute, you could forget France for a thousand years!

LEDUC. I agree. But that does not require an understanding of anything—it is simply faith in the Red Army.

BAYARD. It is faith in the future; and the future is Socialist. And that is what *I* take in there with *me*. *(To the others.)* I warn you—I've had experience with these types. You'd better ram a viewpoint up your spine or you'll break in half.

LEDUC. *(Sensing an ally after all.)* I misunderstood you. You mean it's important not to feel alone, is that it?

BAYARD. None of us is alone. We're members of history. Some of us don't know it, but you'd better learn it for your own preservation.

LEDUC. That we are…symbols.

BAYARD. *(Uncertain whether to agree.)* Yes. Why not? Symbols, yes.

LEDUC. And you feel that helps you?—Believe me, I am genuinely interested.

BAYARD. It helps me because it's the truth. What am I to them personally? Do they know me? You react personally to this, they'll turn you into an idiot. You can't make sense of this on a personal basis.

LEDUC. I agree. *(Personally.)* But the difficulty is—what can one be if not oneself? For example—the thought of torture or something of that sort—

BAYARD. *(Struggling to live his conviction.)* Well, it frightens me—of course. But they can't torture the future; it's out of their hands. Man was not made to be the slave of Big Business. Whatever they do, something inside me is laughing. Because they can't win. Impossible. *(He has stiffened himself against his rising fear.)*

LEDUC. So that in a sense…it's almost that you aren't here. You personally.

BAYARD. *(As though sensing a trap.)* In a sense. Why, what's wrong with that?

LEDUC. Nothing; right now it may be the best way to hold on to oneself. It's just that normally one tries to experience life, to *be* in spirit where one's body is. It's hard to try to be an abstraction.

BAYARD. *(Solicitously.)* You think a man can ever be himself in this society? When millions go hungry and a few live like kings, and whole races are slaves to the stock market—how can you be yourself in such a world? I put in ten hours a day for a few francs, I see people who never bend their backs and they own the planet… how can my spirit be where my body is? I'd have to be an ape…

VON BERG. Then where is your spirit?

BAYARD. In the future. In the day when the working class is master of the world. *That's* my confidence… *(To Monceau.)* not some borrowed personality.

VON BERG. *(Wide-eyed, genuinely asking.)* But don't you think… excuse me. Are not most of the Nazis…of the working class?

BAYARD. Well, naturally, with enough propaganda you can confuse anybody.

VON BERG. I see. *(Slight pause.)* But in that case how can one have such confidence in them?

BAYARD. Who do you have confidence in, the aristocracy?

VON BERG. Very little. But in certain aristocrats, yes. And in certain ordinary people.

BAYARD. Are you telling me that history is a question of "certain people"? Is any of us an individual to them? Class interest makes history, not individuals.

VON BERG. Yes. That seems to be the trouble.

BAYARD. Facts are not trouble. A human being has to glory in the facts. *(To the others.)* I warn you, without a viewpoint you'll…

VON BERG. *(With a deep, anxious outreaching to Bayard.)* But the facts…dear sir, what if the facts are dreadful? And will always be dreadful?

BAYARD. So is childbirth, so is…

VON BERG. But a child comes of it. What if nothing will ever come of the facts but endless, endless disaster? Believe me, I am happy to meet a man who is not cynical; any faith is precious these days. But to give your faith to a…a class of people is impossible, simply impossible—ninety-nine percent of the Nazis are ordinary working-class people!

BAYARD. I concede it *is* possible to propagandize…

VON BERG. *(With an untoward anxiety, as though the settlement of this issue is intimate with him.)* But who can *not* be propagandized? Isn't that the…the only point? A few individuals. Don't you think so?

BAYARD. You're an intelligent man, Prince—are you seriously telling me that five, ten, a thousand, ten thousand decent people are all that stand between us and the end of everything? You mean this whole world is going to hang on that thread?

VON BERG. *(Struck.)* I'm afraid it does seem unlikely.

BAYARD. If I thought that, I wouldn't have the strength to walk through that door, I wouldn't know how to put one foot in front of the other.

VON BERG. *(Slight pause.)* Yes. I hadn't really considered it that way. *(Wanting Bayard's faith.)* But…you really think the working class will…?

BAYARD. They will destroy Fascism because it is against their interest.

VON BERG. *(Nods.)* But then, isn't it even more of a mystery?

BAYARD. I see no mystery.

VON BERG. But they adore Hitler.

BAYARD. How can you say that? Hitler is the creation of the capitalist class.

VON BERG. *(In terrible mourning and anxiety.)* But they adore him! My own cook, my gardeners, the people who work in my forests, the chauffeur, the gamekeeper—they are *Nazis*! I saw it coming over them, their love for this creature—my housekeeper used to dream of him in her bed, she'd serve my breakfast as though a god had slept with her; in a dream burning my toast! I saw this adoration in my own house!—That, that is the dreadful "fact." *(Controlling himself.)* I beg your pardon, but it disturbs me. I admire your faith; all faith to some degree is beautiful. But when I know that yours is based on something so untrue—it's terribly disturbing. *(Quietly.)* In any case, I cannot glory in the facts; there is no reassurance there. They adore him, the salt of the earth... *(Staring.)* adore him.

(There is a burst of laughter from within the office. He glances there, as they all do.)

Strange, if I did not know that most of them in there are French, I'd have said they laugh like Germans. I suppose vulgarity has no nation, after all.

FERRAND. *(Emerging from the office.)* Very true, Captain—good morning, Captain.

(Mr. Ferrand, laughing, shuts the office door, within the laughter is subsiding. He goes past the Waiter.)

THE WAITER. *(Sotto.)* Did you ask about me?

(Ferrand glances back at the door, then quickly leans over and whispers hurriedly into his ear. They all watch. Now Ferrand starts away. The Waiter reaches out and grasps his apron.) Ferrand!

FERRAND. *(Brushing the Waiter's hand off his apron.)* What can I do? I told you fifty times to get out of this city! Didn't I? *(Starting to weep.)* Didn't I?

(He hurries up the corridor, wiping his tears with his apron. They all watch the Waiter, who sits there staring.)

BAYARD. What? Tell me. Come on, I'm next, what'd he say?

THE WAITER. *(A whisper, staring ahead in shock.)* It's not to work.

LEDUC. *(Leaning over toward him to hear.)* What?

THE WAITER. They have furnaces.

BAYARD. What furnaces? ...Talk! What is it?

THE WAITER. He heard the detectives; they came in for coffee just before. People get burned up in furnaces. It's not to work. They burn you up in Poland. All the Jews are burned up.

(Silence. A long moment passes.)

MONCEAU. That is the most fantastic idiocy I ever heard in my life.

LEBEAU. *(To the Waiter.)* As long as you've got real French papers, though...there's nothing about Jew on *my* papers.

THE WAITER. *(In a loud whisper.)* They're going to look at your penis.

(The Boy stands up as though with an electric shock. The Old Jew makes an abortive gesture of protection toward him. The door of the office opens, the Captain of Police appears and beckons to Bayard. The Boy quickly sits.)

POLICE CAPTAIN. You can come now.

(Bayard stands, assuming an artificially and almost absurd posture of confidence. But approaching the Captain he achieves an authority.)

BAYARD. I'm a Head Electrician on the railway, Captain. You may have seen me there. I'm classified First Priority War Worker.

POLICE CAPTAIN. Inside.

BAYARD. *(Bends and ties his shoelace.)* You can check with Transport Minister Duquesne.

POLICE CAPTAIN. Are you trying to tell me my business?

BAYARD. *(With a glance at Monceau.)* No, but we can all use advice from time to time.

POLICE CAPTAIN. Inside.

BAYARD. Right.

(Without hesitation Bayard walks into the office, the Captain following and closing the door. A long silence. Monceau, after a moment, smooths out a rough place on the felt on his hat. Lebeau looks at his papers, slowly rubbing his beard with the back of his hand, staring in terror. The Old Jew draws his bundle deeper under his feet. Leduc takes out a nearly empty pack of cigarettes, starts to take one for himself, then silently stands and crosses the line of men, offers it to them. Lebeau takes one. They light up. Faintly, from the next-door building, an accordion is heard playing a popular tune.)

LEBEAU. Trust a bloody policeman to play an accordion at a time like this.

THE WAITER. No, that's the patron's son, Maurice. They're starting to serve lunch.

(Leduc, who has returned to his position as the last man on the bench, cranes around the corner of the corridor, observes, and sits back.)

LEDUC. *(Quietly.)* Is that the only guard at the door? If that's the only guard, three men could handle him.

(Pause. No one responds. Then...)

VON BERG. *(Apologetically.)* I'm afraid I'd only get in your way. I have a weak heart.

MONCEAU. *(To Leduc.)* You actually believe that, Doctor? About the furnaces?

LEDUC. *(Thinks, then...)* I believe it is possible, yes...would you be willing to try something?

MONCEAU. But what good are dead Jews to them? They want free labor. It's senseless. You can say whatever you like, but the Germans are not illogical; there's no conceivable advantage for them in such a thing.

LEDUC. Good God, man, you can be sitting here and still speak of logic and advantages? Is there really a logical explanation for you sitting here? But you are sitting here, aren't you?

MONCEAU. But an atrocity like that is...beyond belief.

VON BERG. That is exactly the point.

MONCEAU. *(With sinking heart, surprise.)* You don't believe it. Prince, you can't tell me you believe such a thing.

VON BERG. I find it the most believable atrocity I have heard.

LEBEAU. But why?

VON BERG. *(Slight pause.)* Because it *is* so inconceivably vile. That is their power. To do the inconceivable; it paralyzes the rest of us. *(He is almost surprised at finding himself so caught up. He hesitates, then goes on.)* But if that is its purpose it is not the cause. Many times I used to ask my friends—if you love your country why is it necessary to hate other countries? To be a good German why must you despise everything that is not German? Until I realized the answer. They do these things not because they are German but because they are nothing. It is the hallmark of the age—the less you exist the more important it is to make a clear impression. *(Again he stops. But he cannot keep silent.)* I can see them discussing it as a kind of…truthfulness. After all, what *is* self-restraint but hypocrisy? If you despise Jews the most honest thing is to burn them up! And the fact that it costs money, and uses up trains and personnel— this only guarantees the integrity, the purity, the existence of their "feelings"; they would even tell you that only a Jew would think of the cost. They are poets, they are striving for a new nobility, the nobility of the totally vulgar. I believe in this fire; it would prove for all time that they exist, yes, and that they were sincere. You must not calculate these people with some nineteenth-century arithmetic of loss and gain. Their motives are musical and people are merely sounds they play. And in my opinion, win or lose this war, they have pointed the way to the future. What one used to conceive a human being to be will have no room on this earth. *(To the Waiter.)* I would try anything to escape.

(A pause.)

MONCEAU. But they arrested you. That German professor is an expert. There is nothing Jewish about you…

VON BERG. I have an accent. I noticed he reacted when I started to speak. It is an Austrian inflection. *(With an ironical laugh.)* He may think I am another refugee.

(The door opens, the Professor comes out, indicates the Waiter.)

PROFESSOR. Next. You.

(The Waiter makes himself small, pressing up against Lebeau.)

Don't be alarmed, it's only to check your papers. Come on.

(The Waiter suddenly bends over and runs around the corner and up the corridor. The Guard appears at the end and collars him, and carries him, struggling desperately, down the corridor.)

THE WAITER. *(To the Guard.)* Felix, you know me! Felix, my wife will go off her head. Felix…you know me!!

PROFESSOR. Take him in the office.

(The Captain of Police hurries in from the office.)

GUARD. *(Holding the struggling Waiter.)* There's nobody at the door.

POLICE CAPTAIN. Go on—get back. *(Grabs the Waiter from the Guard.)* Get in here, you Jew son-of-a-bitch…

(He throws the Waiter into the office, the Waiter colliding with the Major, who is just coming out to see what the disturbance is. The Major grips his thigh in pain, pushing the Waiter clear. The Waiter slides to the Major's feet, weeping pleadingly.)

THE WAITER. Major!

(The Captain violently jerks him to his feet and pushes him into the office, going in after him. The Major takes out a hip flask and drinks. The Waiter is heard crying out, the sound of blows struck. Quiet. The Professor starts toward the door. The Major takes his arm and leads him down to the extreme forward edge of the stage, out of hearing of the prisoners.)

MAJOR. Professor, wouldn't it be much simpler if you just asked them?

(Impatiently, without replying, the Professor goes over to the line of prisoners.)

PROFESSOR. Are any of you ready to admit right away that you are carrying forged identification papers? *(Silence.)* So. In short, you are all *bona fide* Frenchmen.

(Silence. He goes over to the Old Jew, bends into his face.) Are there any Jews among you?!

(Silence. Then he returns to the Major.) There's the problem, Major; either we go from house to house investigating everyone's biography, or we make this inspection.

MAJOR. That electrician fellow just now, though—I thought he had a good point. In fact, only this morning in the hospital, while I was waiting my turn for X-ray, another officer, a German officer, a captain, in fact—his dressing gown happened to fall open…

PROFESSOR. It is entirely possible.

MAJOR. It was unmistakable, Professor.

PROFESSOR. Let us be clear, Major; the Race Institute does not claim that circumcision is conclusive proof of Jewish blood. The Race Institute recognizes that a small proportion of gentiles…

MAJOR. I see no reason not to say it—I happen to be, myself.

PROFESSOR. Very well, but I certainly would never mistake you for a Jew. Any more than you could mistake a pig for a horse. Science is

36

not capricious, Major; my degree is in racial anthropology. In any case, we can certainly separate the gentiles by this kind of examination. Major? *(He has taken the Major's arm to lead him back to the office.)*

MAJOR. Excuse me. I'll be back in a few minutes. *(Moving to leave.)* You can carry on without me…

PROFESSOR. Major, you are in command of this operation. I must insist you take your place beside me.

MAJOR. I think some mistake has been made. I am a line officer, I have no experience with things of this kind. My training is engineering and artillery.

PROFESSOR. *(Slight pause; he speaks more quietly, his eyes ablaze.)* We'd better be candid, Major; are you refusing this assignment?

MAJOR. *(Registers the threat he feels.)* I'm in pain today, Professor. They are still removing fragments. In fact, I understood I was only filling in here until an S.S. officer took over. I'm more or less on loan, you see, from the regular Army.

PROFESSOR. *(Taking his arm, drawing him down to the edge of the stage again.)* But the Army is not exempt from carrying out the Racial Program. My orders come from the top. And my report will go to the top. You understand me.

MAJOR. *(His resistance seems to fall.)* I do, yes.

PROFESSOR. Look now, if you wish to be relieved, I can easily telephone General Von…

MAJOR. No—no, that's all right… I…I'll be back in a few minutes.

PROFESSOR. This is bizarre, Major—how long am I supposed to wait for you?

MAJOR. *(Holding back an outburst of resentment.)* I need a walk, I am not used to sitting in an office. I see nothing bizarre in it, I am a line officer and this kind of business takes a little getting used to. *(Through his teeth.)* What do you find bizarre in it?

PROFESSOR. Very well.

MAJOR. *(Slight pause.)* I'll be back in ten minutes. You can carry on.

PROFESSOR. I will not continue without you, Major. The Army's responsibility is quite as great as mine here.

MAJOR. I won't be long.

(He turns quickly, very much wanting to get out. Leduc stands as he passes.)

LEDUC. Major...

(The Major strides past him without turning, up the corridor and out. The Professor goes into the office and shuts the door. Silence.)

THE BOY. Doctor? (Leduc turns to him.) I'd try it with you.

LEDUC. (To Monceau and Lebeau.) What about you two?

LEBEAU. Whatever you say, but I'm so hungry I wouldn't do you much good.

LEDUC. You can walk up to him and start an argument, can't you? Distract his attention. Then we...

MONCEAU. You're out of your mind, they'll shoot you down.

LEDUC. Some of us might make it. There's only one guard at the door. This district is full of alleyways—you could disappear in twenty yards.

MONCEAU. How long would you be free?—An hour? And when they catch you they'll really fill you in.

THE BOY. (Angering at Monceau.) Please. I've got to get out. I was on my way to the pawnshop. (Takes out a ring.) It's my mother's wedding ring, it's all that's left. She's waiting for the money. They have nothing in the house to eat.

MONCEAU. You take my advice, boy; don't do anything, they'll let you go.

LEDUC. Like the electrician?

MONCEAU. He was obviously a Communist. And the waiter irritated the Captain.

LEBEAU. Look, I'll try it with you but don't expect too much; I'm weak as a chicken, I haven't eaten since yesterday.

LEDUC. (To Monceau.) It would be better with another man. The boy is very light. If you and the boy rush him I'll get his gun away.

MONCEAU. (Springing up, he goes to a box, sits.) I am not going to risk my life for nothing. That businessman had a Jewish face. (To Lebeau.) You said so yourself.

LEBEAU. *(To Leduc, appeasingly.)* I did. I thought so. Look, if your papers are good maybe that's it.

LEDUC. *(To Lebeau and Monceau—still striving for persuasiveness.)* You know yourself the Germans have been moving into the Southern Zone; you see they are picking up Jews; a man has just told you that you are marked for destruction…

MONCEAU. *(Indicates Von Berg.)* They took him in. Nobody's explained it.

VON BERG. My accent…

MONCEAU. My dear Prince, you're obviously an Austrian of the upper class. I took you for nobility the minute you walked in. *(To Leduc.)* It's a general check-up!

LEDUC. Then why would they be looking at penises?

MONCEAU. There's no evidence of that!

LEDUC. The waiter's boss…

MONCEAU. *(Nearing a nervous shout.)* He overheard two French detectives who can't possibly know anything about what happens in Poland. And if they do do that kind of thing it's not the end, either—I had Jew stamped on my passport in Paris and I was playing Cyrano at the same time.

VON BERG. Really!—Cyrano!

LEBEAU. Then why'd you leave Paris?

MONCEAU. It was an absolutely idiotic accident. I was sharing a flat with another actor, a gentile. And he kept warning me to get out. They're terribly vicious with gentiles who help Jews, you know. But naturally one doesn't just give up a role like that. But finally I decided to at least get rid of certain books that were on the forbidden list—of Communistic literature—Sinclair Lewis, and Thomas Mann, and even a few things by Friedrich Engels, which everybody was reading at one time. So we made bundles and as the flat was on the fifth floor, we'd take turns going down to the street and just leaving them on benches or in doorways or anywhere at all. It was after midnight, and I was just dropping a bundle into the gutter near the Opera, when I noticed a man standing in a doorway watching me. At that moment I realized that I had stamped my name and address in every one of those books.

VON BERG. Hah! What did you do?

MONCEAU. Started walking, and kept going until I got to the Unoccupied Zone. *(Suppressing an outcry of remorse.)* But in my opinion, if I'd done nothing at all I might still be working!

LEDUC. *(With higher urgency, but deeply sympathetic, to Monceau.)* Listen to me for one moment. I beg you. There is only one man guarding that door; you heard him say so; we may never get another chance like this again.

LEBEAU. That's another thing; if it was all that serious wouldn't they be guarding us more heavily? I mean that's a point.

LEDUC. That is exactly the point. They are relying on us.

MONCEAU. Relying on us!

LEDUC. Yes. To project our own reasonable ideas into each other's heads. It *is* reasonable that a light guard means the thing is not important. They rely on our own logic to immobilize ourselves.

MONCEAU. Oh, really.

LEDUC. Listen to your feelings, not your logic. You have just told us how you went all over Paris advertising the fact that you owned forbidden books…

MONCEAU. But I didn't do it purposely!

LEDUC. May I guess that you could no longer stand the strain of remaining in Paris? But you couldn't bear to lose your Cyrano, either? So your subconscious broke the logjam; despite yourself it forced you into the street and saved your life! Rely on what you know, not on what you think. And surely you know the danger here!

MONCEAU. *(In high anxiety.)* I played in Germany. That audience could not burn up actors in a furnace. *(Turning to Von Berg—half-pleading, half-demanding.)* Prince, you cannot tell me you believe that!

VON BERG. *(After a pause.)* I supported a small orchestra. When the Germans came into Austria three of the players prepared to escape. I convinced them no harm would come to them; I brought them to my castle; we all lived together. The oboist was twenty, twenty-one—the heart stopped when he played certain tones. They came for him in the garden. They took him out of his chair. The instrument lay on the lawn like a dead bone. I made certain inquiries; he is dead now. And it was even more terrible—they came and sat down and listened until the rehearsal was over. And then they took him. It is as though they wished to take him at exactly the moment when he was most beautiful. I know how you feel—but I tell you nothing any longer is forbidden. Nothing. *(Tears are in his eyes, he turns away.)*

(Pause.)

THE BOY. Will they let you go?

VON BERG. I suppose. If this is all to catch Jews they will let me go.

THE BOY. Would you take this ring? And bring it back to my mother? *(He stretches his hand out with the ring. Von Berg does not touch it.)* Number 9 Rue Charlot. Top floor. Hirsch. Sarah Hirsch. She has long brown hair...be sure it's her. She has a little beauty spot on this cheek. There are two other families in the apartment so be sure it's her.

(Von Berg looks into the Boy's face. Then he turns to Leduc.)

VON BERG. Come. Tell me what to do. I'll try to help you. *(To Leduc.)* Doctor?

LEDUC. I'm afraid it's hopeless.

VON BERG. Why?

LEDUC. *(Stares ahead, then looks at Lebeau.)* He says he's weak with hunger, and the boy's like a feather. I wanted to get away, not just be slaughtered. *(Pause; with bitter irony.)* I live in the country, you see; it's so long since I talked to anybody, I'm afraid I came in here with the wrong assumptions.

MONCEAU. If you're trying to bait me, Doctor, you're wasting your time.

LEDUC. Can I ask you something, are you religious?

MONCEAU. Not at all.

LEDUC. Then why do you feel this desire to be sacrificed?

MONCEAU. I ask you to stop talking to me!

LEDUC. Dear man, you are making a gift of yourself. You are the only able-bodied man here, aside from me, and yet you feel no impulse to do something? *(Angering.)* Where do you get this air of confidence!

MONCEAU. *(His back to the wall.)* I refuse to play a part I do not fit. Everyone is playing the victim these days; hopeless, hysterical, they always assume the worst. I have papers; I will present them with the single idea that they must be honored. I think that is exactly what saved that businessman. You accuse us of acting the part the Germans created for us; I think you're the one who's doing that by acting so desperately.

LEDUC. And if, despite your act, they throw you into a freight car?

MONCEAU. I don't think they will.

LEDUC. But if they do. You certainly have enough imagination to visualize that.

MONCEAU. *(Desperately.)* In that case I will have done my best. I know what failure is; it took me a long time to make good; I haven't the personality for leading roles; everyone said I was crazy to stay in the profession. But I did, and I imposed my idea on others.

LEDUC. In other words, you will create yourself.

MONCEAU. *(Again, almost secure.)* Every actor creates himself.

LEDUC. But when they tell you to open your fly.

(Monceau is silent, furious.) Please don't stop now; I'm very interested. How do you regard that moment?

(Monceau is silent.) I am incapable of penetrating such passivity; I ask you what is in your mind when you face the command to open your fly. I am being as impersonal, as scientific as I know how to be—I believe I am going to be murdered. What do you believe will happen when they point to that spot between your legs?

(Pause.)

MONCEAU. *(Stiffly.)* I have nothing to say to you.

LEBEAU. I'll tell you what I'll feel. *(Indicates Von Berg.)* I'll wish I was him.

LEDUC. To be someone else.

LEBEAU. *(Exhausted.)* Yes. To have been arrested by mistake. God!—To see them relaxing when they realize I am innocent.

LEDUC. *(As though Lebeau's resistance is possible.)* You feel guilty, then.

LEBEAU. A little, I suppose. Not for anything I've done but… I don't know why.

LEDUC. For being a Jew, perhaps?

LEBEAU. I'm not ashamed of being a Jew.

LEDUC. Then why feel guilty?

LEBEAU. I don't know. Maybe it's that they keep saying such terrible things about us, and you can't answer. And after years and years of it, you… I wouldn't say you believe it, but…you do, a little. It's a funny thing—I used to say to my mother and father just what you're saying. We could have gone to America a month before the war. But they wouldn't leave Paris. She had this brass bed, and carpets, and draperies and all kinds of trash. Just like him with his Cyrano. And I told them, "You're doing just what they want you to do!" But people won't believe they can be killed, you know. Them with their brass bed and their carpets and their faces…

LEDUC. But do you believe it? It seems to me you don't believe it yourself.

LEBEAU. I believe it. They only caught me this morning because I… I always used to walk in the morning before I sat down to work. And I wanted to do it again. I knew I shouldn't go outside. But you get tired of believing the truth. You get tired of seeing things clearly. *(Pause.)* I always collected my illusions in the morning. I could never paint what I saw, only what I imagined. And this morning, danger or no danger, I just had to get out, to walk around, to see something real, something but the inside of my head…and I hardly turned the…corner and that little schmuck of a scientist got out of the car with his fingers going for my nose… *(Pause.)* I believe I can die. But you can get so tired…

LEDUC. That it's not too bad.

LEBEAU. Almost, yes.

LEDUC. *(Glancing at them all.)* So that one way or the other, with illusions or without them, exhausted or fresh—we have been trained to die. *(Especially to Monceau.)* The Jew and the gentile both.

MONCEAU. You're still trying to bait me, Doctor, but if you want to commit suicide do it alone, don't involve others. The fact is there are laws and every government enforces its laws; and I want it understood that I have nothing to do with any of this talk!

LEDUC. *(Angering now.)* Every government does not have laws condemning people because of their race...

MONCEAU. I beg your pardon. The Russians condemn the Jews and the middle class, the English have condemned the Irish, Africans, and anybody else they could lay their hands on; the French, the Italians...every nation has condemned somebody because of his race; look at the Americans and what they do to Negroes. The vast majority of mankind is condemned because of its race. What do you advise all these people—suicide?

LEDUC. What do you advise?

MONCEAU. I go on the assumption that if I obey the law with dignity I will live in peace. I may not like the law; but evidently the majority does or they would overthrow it. And I'm speaking now of the French majority who outnumber the Germans in this town fifty to one. These are French police, don't forget, not German. And if by some miracle you did knock out that guard and escape you would find yourself in a city where not one person in a thousand would help you. And it's got nothing to do with being Jewish or not Jewish. It is what the world is, so why don't you stop insulting others with romantic challenges!

LEDUC. In short, because the world is indifferent you will wait calmly and with great dignity—to open your fly.

MONCEAU. *(Frightened and furious, he stands.)* I'll tell you what I think; I think it's people like you who brought this on us. People who give Jews a reputation for subversion, and this Talmudic analysis, and this everlasting niggling, discontent.

LEDUC. Then I will tell you that I was wrong before. You didn't advertise your name on those forbidden books in order to find a reason to leave Paris and save yourself. It was in order to get yourself caught and be put out of your misery. Your heart is conquered territory.

MONCEAU. If we meet again you will pay for that remark.

LEDUC. Conquered territory!

(The Boy suddenly stands and starts up the corridor. Leduc reaches out and stops him.) Where are you going?

(The Boy impatiently frees himself from Leduc and steps over to Von Berg, offering him the ring.)

THE BOY. Will you do it? Number 9 Rue Charlot.

(Von Berg, astonished, accepts the ring. The Boy without hesitation again starts up the corridor. Leduc goes quickly to him.)

LEDUC. Wait a minute!

(He reaches the Boy and they whisper together as Leduc takes out a clasp knife and opens the blade. The Boy nods agreement. They face the corridor. Leduc conceals the knife in his hand. Von Berg, meanwhile, softly sings Brahms' Lullaby, as though to add a covering to their escape.)

MONCEAU. *(Clearing a space away from them.)* You're out of your mind. Out of your mind!

(Leduc and the Boy start up the corridor. Von Berg sings on. A few yards up Leduc suddenly begins to yell.)

LEDUC. Guard! Hey! Guard! Guard! Come quick! Guard!

(The Guard appears, running toward them.)

GUARD. What? What?

LEDUC. Come quick!

(Drawing his revolver the Guard starts into the detention room with Leduc, while the Boy is slipping away up the corridor. The Guard, realizing, turns with a shout toward the Boy, and Leduc is raising his knife behind the Guard's back, when the Major appears at the head of the corridor, the Boy halted by the sight of him. Leduc quickly pockets the knife. The Major is drunk, his walk is unsteady. The Boy turns and comes back down the corridor as the Major asks the Guard…)

MAJOR. What's the boy doing up here?

GUARD. *(Indicating Leduc.)* Sir, this man…

MAJOR. Get back on the door.

(The Guard glares at Leduc, then goes up past the Major and disappears. The Major comes to Leduc, who is waiting for the consequences.

The Major is "high"—with drink and a flow of emotion.)

That's impossible. There are sentries on both corners. *(Glancing toward the office door.)* Captain, I would only like to say that…this is all as inconceivable to me as it is to you. Can you believe that? *(In despair for himself and the relief of the despairing, the ironical letting-go.)*

LEDUC. I'd believe it if you shot yourself. And better yet, if you took a few of them with you.

MAJOR. *(Wiping his mouth with the back of his hand.)* We would all be replaced by tomorrow morning, wouldn't we?

LEDUC. *(Surprised the Major has even replied.)* We might get out alive, though; you could see to that.

MAJOR. They'd find you soon.

LEDUC. Not me.

MAJOR. *(With a manic amusement, covering a deeply questioning agony.)* Why do you deserve to live more than I do?

LEDUC. *(With a shred of hope.)* Because I am incapable of doing what you are doing. I am better for the world than you.

MAJOR. It means nothing to you that I have feelings about this?

LEDUC. Nothing whatever, unless you get us out of here.

MAJOR. *(His sympathy refused, a trace of sharp irony hardens his voice.)* And then what? Then what?

LEDUC. I will remember a decent German, an honorable German.

MAJOR. *(His irony sharper, but it seems to reveal suffering as well as anger.)* Will that make a difference?

LEDUC. I will love you as long as I live. Will anyone do that now?

MAJOR. That means so much to you?—That someone loves you?

LEDUC. That I be worthy of someone's love, yes. And respect.

MAJOR. It's amazing; you don't understand anything. Nothing of that kind is left, don't you understand that yet?

LEDUC. It is left in me.

MAJOR. *(More loudly, a fury rising in him.)* There are no persons anymore, don't you see that? There will never be persons again. What do I care if you love me? Are you out of your mind? *(Roar-*

46

ing.) What am I, a dog that I must be loved? You… *(Turning to all of them.)* bloody Jews!

(The door opens, the Professor and Police Captain appear.)

Like dogs, Jew-dogs. Look at him… *(The Old Jew.)* with his paws folded. Look what happens when I yell at him. Dog! He doesn't move. Does he move? Do you see him moving?! But we move, don't we? We measure your noses, don't we, Herr Professor, and we look at your penises, we keep moving continually!

PROFESSOR. *(With a gesture to draw him inside.)* Major…

MAJOR. Hands off, you civilian bastard, shut up!

PROFESSOR. I think…you'd better come… *(Again reaches for the Major's arm.)*

MAJOR. *(Drawing his revolver.)* Not a word!

PROFESSOR. *(Backing quickly from the sight of the drawn gun.)* You're drunk.

(The Major fires into the ceiling. The prisoners tense in shock. He looks in astonishment at his own gun.)

MAJOR. Everything stops now.

(He staggers, but with strange concentration, revolver cocked in his hand, and falls into a sitting position on the bench beside Lebeau.) Now it is all stopped.

(His hands are shaking. He sniffs in his running nose. He crosses his legs to control them, and he looks at Leduc.) Now you tell me. You tell me. Now nothing is moving. You tell me. Go ahead now.

LEDUC. *(Aware of the gun.)* What shall I tell you?

MAJOR. Tell me how…how there can be persons anymore. I have you at the end of this revolver. *(Indicates the Professor, hefting the gun.)* —He has me—and somebody has him—and somebody else has somebody else. Now tell me.

LEDUC. I told you.

MAJOR. I won't repeat it. I am a man of honor. *(Starting up, going to Leduc.)* What do you make of that? I will not tell them what you tried just now—or what you advised me to do. What do you say— damned decent of me, isn't it…not to repeat your advice.

(Leduc is silent. Major is close now to Leduc in a corner of the stage. Pause.)

Were you on active service?

LEDUC. Yes.

MAJOR. No record of subversive activities against the German Authority.

LEDUC. No.

MAJOR. If you were released, and the others were kept…would you refuse?

(Leduc is silent.)

Would you refuse?

LEDUC. *(Slight pause.)* No.

MAJOR. And walk out of that door with a light heart?

(Leduc is looking at the floor now, angry and deeply ashamed.)

LEDUC. I don't know. *(He starts to put his trembling hands into his pockets.)*

MAJOR. Don't hide your hands. I am trying to understand why you are better for the world than me, why do you hide your hands? *(Leduc frees his hands.)* Would you go out that door with a light heart, run to your woman, drink a toast to your skin? …Why are you better than anybody else?

LEDUC. I have no duty to make a gift of myself to your sadism.

MAJOR. *(Triumphantly.)* But I do? To others' sadism? Of myself? I have that duty and you do not? To make a gift of myself?

(Leduc looks at the Professor and the Captain of Police, glances back at the Major.)

LEDUC. I have nothing to say.

MAJOR. *(Suddenly giving a sharp, comradely jab on the shoulder, a laugh in his voice.)* That's better!

(He puts his gun away, turns, swaying to the Professor, and in deep self-contempt as well as hatred for the Professor…) Next!

(The Major brushes past the Professor into the office.)

PROFESSOR. *(To Lebeau.)* Next.

(Lebeau stands up, starts sleepily toward the corridor, turns about and moves into the office, the Professor following him. Leduc returns to his seat. Police Captain goes into the office. The door shuts.)

MONCEAU. You happy now, Doctor? Now you've made him furious. Are you satisfied?

(Pause. The door opens, the Captain appears, beckons to Monceau.)

MAJOR. *(From within, violently.)* Next!

CAPTAIN. Next.

(Monceau smiles, gets up with a forced leisureliness, swings his muffler around his neck, picks up his hat, and with a smiling flourish says to Von Berg…)

MONCEAU. *Ma panache.*

(He goes into office, calling out quite brightly as he enters…) Good morning, Major! *(Captain, following, shuts the door.)*

THE BOY. What did he mean?

VON BERG. It is the last line of a play he was in—"*Ma panache.*"
(Pause.)

THE BOY. Will you do it? Number 9 Rue Charlot. Please be sure.

VON BERG. I'll be sure.

THE BOY. I'm a minor. I'm not even fifteen. Does it apply to minors?

(Captain opens the door, enters, beckons to the Boy. He stands.)

I'm a minor. I'm not fifteen until February…

CAPTAIN. Inside.

THE BOY. *(Halting before the Captain.)* I could get my birth certificate for you.

CAPTAIN. *(Prodding him along.)* Inside, inside.

(They go in. The door shuts. The accordion is heard again from next door. The Old Jew begins to rock back and forth slightly, praying softly. Von Berg notices him, then turns to Leduc on his other side. The three are alone now.)

VON BERG. Does he realize what is happening?

LEDUC. *(With an edgy note of impatience.)* As much as anyone can, I suppose.

VON BERG. He seems to be watching it all from the stars. *(Slight pause.)* I wish we could have met under other circumstances. There are a great many things I'd like to have asked you.

LEDUC. *(Rapidly, sensing the imminent summons.)* I'd appreciate it if you'd do me a favor.

VON BERG. Certainly.

LEDUC. Will you go and tell my wife?

VON BERG. Where is she?

LEDUC. *(Sketching on his palm with a pen.)* When you get to the main road go north out of town. After about two kilometers you'll see a small forest on the left and a lane leading into it. Go down the lane until you see the river. Follow the river upstream to a small mill. They are in the tool shed behind the wheel.

VON BERG. *(Uncomfortably.)* And...what shall I say?

LEDUC. That I've been arrested. And that there may be a possibility I can... *(Breaks off; with a certain vindictiveness.)* No, tell her the truth.

VON BERG. By which you mean?

LEDUC. The furnaces. Tell her that.

VON BERG. But...that's only a rumor, isn't it?

LEDUC. *(Turns to him—sharply, and with a superfluous anger.)* I don't regard it as a rumor. It should be known. I never heard of it before. It must be known. Just take her aside—there's no need for the children to hear it, but tell her.

VON BERG. It would not be easy for me. To tell such a thing to a woman.

LEDUC. *(Flaring up.)* If it's happening you can find a way to say it, can't you?

VON BERG. *(Hesitates, senses Leduc's resentment.)* Very well. I'll tell her. I have no great...facility with women. But I'll do as you say. *(Pause; he glances to the door.)* They're taking rather longer with that boy. Maybe he is too young, you suppose? *(Leduc does not answer.)* They would stick to the rules, you know...perhaps,

50

with the shortage of doctors you suppose they...?

(He breaks off as Leduc clamps his jaws and impatiently turns away.)

I'm sorry if I said anything to offend you.

LEDUC. *(Struggling with his anger.)* That's all right. *(Slight pause. His voice is trembling.)* It's just that you keep finding these little shreds of hope and it is a little difficult. To put it mildly.

VON BERG. Yes, I see. I beg your pardon. I understand.

(Pause. Leduc glances at the door, he is shifting about in high tension.)

Would you like to talk of something else, perhaps? Are you interested in...the arts?

LEDUC. *(Desperately trying to control himself.)* It's really quite simple. It's that you'll survive, you see.

VON BERG. But how can you blame *me* for that?

LEDUC. I don't know how...but I blame you! Yes. That's how it is. I'm sorry. *(He turns away.)*

VON BERG. Doctor, I can promise you—it will not be easy for me to walk out of here.

(Leduc tries not to reply. Then...)

LEDUC. I'm afraid it will only be difficult because it is so easy.

VON BERG. I think that's unfair.

LEDUC. Well, it doesn't matter.

VON BERG. It does to me. I... I was very close to suicide in Austria. When they murdered my musicians—not that alone, but when I told the story to many of my friends there was hardly any reaction. That was almost worse. Can you understand such indifference?

LEDUC. *(Seems on the verge of an outbreak.)* You're really...quite astounding, you know that?

VON BERG. But if one gives up one's ideals...what *is* there? What is left?

LEDUC. *You* are left. With or without ideals...you are left.

VON BERG. I'm terribly sorry... I understand.

LEDUC. Of course you do. So why go on about it? *(Slight pause.)*

51

Forgive me. I do appreciate your feeling, but it's difficult to listen to sentimentality, even if it's well-meant.

VON BERG. I had no intention of being sentimental.

LEDUC. Oh, you must!—You will survive, you will have to sentimentalize it; just a little; just enough to feel you've "shared" this. It's no reflection on you... *(Slight pause.)* ...but it can still make one furious! It is why this agony is so pointless! We are roaches stepped on in the dark. It can never be a lesson, it can never have a meaning. And it will be repeated again and again forever.

VON BERG. Because it cannot be shared?

LEDUC. Yes; because it cannot be shared. Except to weep... and silently thank God that one was spared.

(Leduc glances at the office door, then leans forward, trying to collect himself against his terror.) How strange—one can even become impatient to get on with it.

VON BERG. Yes!

LEDUC. *(With a groan of anger against himself.)* Hm!—What devils they are.

VON BERG. Yes, they can make death seductive...it is their worst sin. *(He hesitates, then comes closer to Leduc.)* I would like...to tell you something. Perhaps you will despise me, but it has weighed on my mind...and I would like to say it...to you.

(Leduc waits.)

I used to dream at night...of Hitler. In a great flowing cloak. Almost like a gown. Almost like a woman. He was...beautiful! *(Slight pause.)* In fact, even now, sometimes as I close my eyes, he comes to me that way. And I have always had such hatred for him! I have kept myself awake some nights to keep from dreaming. I don't understand it!—From the beginning he was contemptible to me!

LEDUC. Why should I despise you? It's not so easy to know who one hates... *(He is evidently aware of a new thought and breaks off. His tone now conveys a deep, inner fright.)* Listen—don't mention the furnaces to my wife.

VON BERG. I'm so glad you say that, I feel very relieved. It is only a rumor, after all...

(Leduc moves, deeply agitated, searching out a unity for his fragmented thought.)

LEDUC. Yes, of course it is—I don't know what got into me—don't mention it, please.

(Very slight pause. He speaks as though a new dreadful image of himself were forming before his eyes.)

You see, she suddenly got a terrible toothache. It went on for days. I thought I might find some codein in the city. But it meant exposing myself when we have such a perfect hideout. And in a way it was senseless... I knew it when I walked down the road! *(Angering despite himself.)* To be risking so much for a goddam toothache... *(With an indignant blow against his chest.)* I would never have asked it for myself... I'd not have allowed it! So what if she doesn't sleep for a couple of weeks! I knew they'd be after the Jews one of these days. I knew it! And she knew it!

VON BERG. Yes, but if one loves someone... *(Breaks off. Pause.)*

LEDUC. *(The total collapse of meaning is in his tone.)* We are not in love anymore. It's just too difficult to separate in these times with the children so small.

VON BERG. *(Sensing the void in Leduc.)* Oh, how terrible.

LEDUC. But don't mention the furnaces. Please. *(With great self-contempt.)* God, at a time like this—to think of taking vengeance on *her*!—What scum we are!

(Pause.)

VON BERG. Does she have sufficient money?

LEDUC. You could help her that way if you like. Thank you. *(He hesitates, then comes close to Von Berg.)* Listen to me—I want you to tell her—that I will find some way to get back. She is not to worry herself or the children. Tell her that I will...I will try to change every-thing...between us. That she was not altogether at fault. I have been intolerant. And arrogant. She is not to feel it was all meaningless— *(Breaks off.)* Just say that. *(Turns to Von Berg.)* Can you?

VON BERG. *(Quickly assuring Leduc of his feeling.)* Oh, yes!

(His need is growing desperate in him, he even wanders unwittingly toward the office door.)

Do you suppose if I offered him something? I can get hold of a good deal of money.—I know so little about people...

LEDUC. You might feel him out, though—try it.

VON BERG. (*Asking advice.*) But he seems rather an idealist, it could infuriate him against me.

LEDUC. I...I don't know. You mustn't endanger yourself. It would be stupid.

VON BERG. What shall I do?—How upside-down everything is—to find oneself wishing for a money-loving cynic!

LEDUC. Why not? We've learned the fraud of idealism, haven't we?

VON BERG. (*Near the peak of his anxiety, his new vision of himself, and in the anguish of his search he nearly cries out.*) But can one really wish for a world without ideals? (*Leduc stands motionless.*) Is there really nothing?—Is that it? For you...there is nothing?

LEDUC. (*Flying out at him.*) Are you asking me to discuss *ideals*? You dare to speak that word on this planet...again?! Are you an idiot or a liar!

MAJOR. (*Unseen within the office.*) Next!

(*The door opens. The Professor enters, comes D. glancing at Von Berg and Leduc, then at the Old Jew. He seems upset, by an argument he had in the office, possibly.*)

PROFESSOR. Next. Next. (*Lights cigarette.*) Next.

(*The Old Jew does not turn to him.*)

You hear me, why do you sit there? Come on.

(*He strides to the Old Jew and lifts him to his feet brusquely. The man reaches down to pick up his bundle, but the Professor tries to push it back to the floor.*) Leave that.

(*With a wordless little cry, the Old Jew clings to his bundle.*) Leave it!

(*The Professor strikes at the Old Jew's hand, but he only holds on tighter, uttering his wordless little cries. The Police Captain comes out as the Professor pulls at the bundle and joins the struggle.*) Let go of that!

(*The bundle rips open. A white cloud of feathers blows up out of it. For an instant everything stops as the Professor looks in surprise at the feathers floating down. The Major appears in the doorway as the feathers settle.)*

POLICE CAPTAIN. Come on.

(The Captain and the Professor lift the Old Jew and carry him past the Major into the office. The Major with deadened eyes glances at the feathers and limps in, closing the door behind him. Leduc and Von Berg stare at the feathers, some of which have fallen on them. They silently brush them off. Leduc picks the last one off his jacket, opens his fingers, and lets it fall to the floor. Silence. Suddenly a short burst of laughter is heard from the office.)

VON BERG. *(With great difficulty, not looking at Leduc.)* I would like to be able to part with your friendship. Is that possible?

LEDUC. *(Pause.)* Prince, in my profession one gets the habit of looking at oneself quite impersonally. It is not you I am angry with. In one part of my mind it is not even this Nazi. I am only angry that I should have been born before the day when man has accepted his own nature; that he is *not* reasonable, that he is full of murder, that his ideals are only the little tax he pays for the right to hate and kill with a clear conscience. I am only angry that knowing this I still deluded myself. That there was not time to truly make part of myself what I know, and to teach others the truth.

VON BERG. *(Angered, above his anxiety.)* There are ideals, Doctor, of another kind. There are people who would find it easier to die than stain one finger with this murder. They exist, I swear it to you. People for whom everything is *not* permitted, foolish people and ineffectual, but they do exist and will not dishonor their tradition. *(Desperately.)* I ask your friendship.

(Again laughter is heard from within the office. This time it is louder. Leduc slowly turns to Von Berg.)

LEDUC. I owe you the truth, Prince; you won't believe it now, but I wish you would think about it and what it means. I have never analyzed a gentile who did not have, somewhere hidden in his mind, a dislike if not a hatred for the Jews.

VON BERG. *(Clapping his ears shut, springing up.)* That is impossible, it is not true of me!

LEDUC. *(Standing, coming to him, a wild pity in his voice.)* Until you know it is true of you you will destroy whatever truth can come of this atrocity. Part of knowing who we are is knowing we are not someone else. And Jew is only the name we give to that stranger, that agony we cannot feel, that death we look at like a cold abstraction. Each man has his Jew; the black, the yellow, the white, it is the other. And the Jews have their Jews. And now, now above all, you must see that you have yours—the man whose death leaves you relieved that you are not him, despite your decency. And that is why there is nothing and will be nothing—until you face your own complicity with this...your own humanity.

VON BERG. I deny that. I deny it absolutely. I have never in my life said a word against your people. Is that your implication? That I have something to do with this monstrousness! I have put a pistol to my head! To my head!

(Laughter is heard again.)

LEDUC. *(Hopelessly.)* I'm sorry; it doesn't really matter.

VON BERG. It matters very much to me. Very much to me!

LEDUC. *(In a level tone full of mourning, and yet behind it a howling terror.)* Prince, you asked me before if I knew your cousin, Baron Kessler.

(Von Berg looks at him, already with anxiety.)

Baron Kessler is a Nazi. He helped to remove all the Jewish doctors from the medical school.

(Von Berg is struck, his eyes glance about.)

You were aware of that, weren't you?

(Half-hysterical laughter comes from the office.)

You must have heard that at some time or another, didn't you?

VON BERG. *(Stunned, inward-seeing.)* Yes. I heard it. I... I had forgotten it. You see, he was...

LEDUC. ...Your cousin. I understand. *(They are quite joined, and Leduc is mourning for the Prince as much as for himself, despite his anger.)* And in any case, it is only a small part of Baron Kessler to you. I do understand it. But it is all of Baron Kessler to me. When you said his name it was with love; and I'm sure he must be a man of some kindness, with whom you can see eye to eye in many things. But when I hear that name I see a knife. You see now why I say there is nothing, and will be nothing, when even you cannot really put yourself in my place? Even you!? And that is why your thoughts of suicide do not move me. It's not your guilt I want, it's your responsibility—that might have helped. Yes, if you had understood that Baron Kessler was in part, in some part, in some small and frightful part—doing your will. You might have done something then, with your standing, and your name and your decency, aside from shooting yourself!

VON BERG. *(In full horror, his face upthrust, calling.)* What can ever save us?! *(He covers his face in his hands.)*

(The door opens. The Professor comes out.)

PROFESSOR. *(Beckoning to the Prince.)* Next.

(Von Berg does not turn, but holds Leduc in his horrified, beseeching gaze. The Professor approaches the Prince.) Come!

(The Professor reaches down to take Von Berg's arm. Von Berg angrily brushes away his abhorrent hand.)

VON BERG. Wagen Sie nicht, mich anzurüren! Hände weg!

(The Professor retracts his hand immobilized, surprised, and for a moment has no strength against his own recognition of authority. Von Berg turns back to Leduc, who glances up at him and smiles with warmth, then turns away. Von Berg turns toward the door and reaching into his breast pocket for a wallet of papers, goes into the office. The Professor follows and closes the door.)

(Alone, Leduc sits motionless. Now he begins the movements of the trapped, he swallows with difficulty, crosses and recrosses his legs. Now he is still again and bends over and cranes around the corner of the corridor to look for the Guard. A movement of his foot stirs up feathers. The accordion is heard outside. He angrily kicks a feather off his foot. Now he makes a decision, and quickly reaching into his pocket, takes out a clasp knife, opens the blade, and begins to get to his feet, starting for the corridor. The door opens and Von Berg comes out. In his hand is a white pass. The door shuts behind him. He is looking at the pass as he goes by Leduc, and reaching the mouth of the corridor he halts. He returns to Leduc.)

Please. Say nothing to me.

(Suddenly he thrusts the pass into Leduc's hand.) Go.

(Leduc looks at the pass then at him, shocked and horrified. He stands.)
Go, go!

LEDUC. What will happen to you!

VON BERG. There is nothing to say. Go!

LEDUC. I wasn't asking you to do this! You don't owe me this!

VON BERG. It isn't you. *(He sits on the bench facing forward, an utter privacy closing upon him. He is trembling, full of fear and wonder.)* Not you at all.

(Leduc, his eyes wide with uncertainty, all but immobilized with guilt, is backing toward the corridor. With a faint cry he turns and hurries away. The Guard appears at the turning of the corridor, receives the pass, and disappears after Leduc. Von Berg, alone, facing front, clasping his hands to subdue their trembling. The office door opens, the Professor appears.)

PROFESSOR. Ne... *(He breaks off, glances about. To Von Berg.)*
Where's your pass?

(Von Berg stares ahead. The Professor dashes to the office and calls inside.) Man escaped!

(He starts running toward the corridor as the Captain of Police rushes out, and calling back to him...indicating Von Berg.) He gave his pass away!

(The Major appears in the office doorway. The Captain of Police runs, following the Professor up the corridor.) Man escaped! Man escaped!

POLICE CAPTAIN. Who let him out! Find that man! The siren! The siren!

(Both are gone, their cries swept away by the siren going off. By this time, the Major has hurried to the corridor where he halts. The siren is moving away in pursuit. The Major turns to Von Berg, murderous fury in his face, his fists clenching. Suddenly he draws his gun, and Von Berg turns to face him, standing. But he only half-raises the weapon as though in terrible conflict.)

58

(Light begins to dim as at the head of the corridor four new men, prisoners, appear. Rapidly herded in by the detectives, they sit on the bench, glancing about at the ceiling, the walls, the feathers on the floor, and the two motionless men. The light is gone out on the new captives, lingering for a fading moment on the Major and Von Berg, who stand there, forever incomprehensible to one another, looking into each other's eyes.)

End of Play

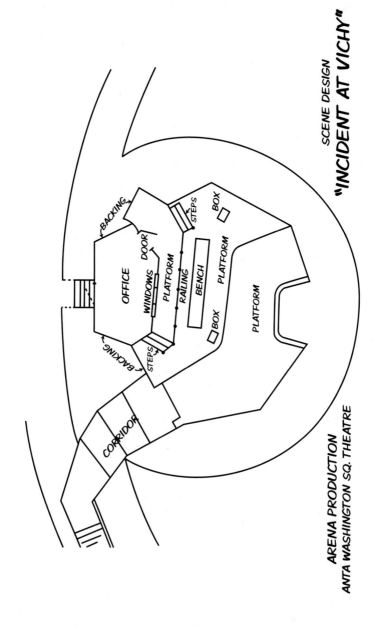

SCENE DESIGN
"INCIDENT AT VICHY"

ARENA PRODUCTION
ANTA WASHINGTON SQ. THEATRE

PROPERTY LIST
(Use this space to create props lists for your production)

SOUND EFFECTS
(Use this space to create sound effects lists for your production)

NOTES
(Use this space to make notes for your production)